COOL

PHYSICAL EVIDENCE

What's Left Behind

ESTHER BECK

ABDO
Publishing Company

VISIT US AT WWW.ABDOPUBLISHING.COM

Published by ABDO Publishing Company, 8000 West 78th Street, Edina, Minnesota 55439.
Copyright © 2009 by Abdo Consulting Group, Inc. International copyrights reserved in all countries.
No part of this book may be reproduced in any form without written permission from the publisher.
The Checkerboard Library™ is a trademark and logo of ABDO Publishing Company.

Printed in the United States.
Design and Production: Mighty Media, Inc.
Art Direction: Kelly Doudna
Photo Credits: Kelly Doudna, Ablestock, iStockPhoto (Brandon Alms, Jeff Chevrier, Gerard Maas, Millanovic, Dragan Trifunovic), ShutterStock
Series Editor: Pam Price
The following manufacturers/names appearing in this book are trademarks: Arm & Hammer, C & H, Calumet, Clabber Girl

Library of Congress Cataloging-in-Publication Data

Beck, Esther.
  Cool physical evidence : what's left behind / Esther Beck.
    p. cm. -- (Cool CSI)
  Includes index.
  ISBN 978-1-60453-487-0
  1. Crime scene searches--Juvenile literature. 2. Forensic science--Juvenile literature. I. Title.

  HV8073.8.B433 2009
  363.25'62--dc22

                              2008023819

TO ADULT HELPERS

You're invited to assist up-and-coming forensic investigators! And it will pay off in many ways. Your children can develop new skills, gain confidence, and do some interesting projects while learning about science. What's more, it's going to be a lot of fun!

These projects are designed to let children work independently as much as possible. Let them do whatever they are able to do on their own. Also encourage them to keep a CSI journal. Soon, they will be thinking like real investigators.

So get out your magnifying glass and stand by. Let your young investigators take the lead. Watch and learn. Praise their efforts. Enjoy the scientific adventure!

CONTENTS

fingerprint

shoe print

fibers

FUN WITH FORENSICS

So you want to know more about crime scene investigation, or CSI. Perhaps you saw a crime solvers show on television and liked it. Or maybe you read about an ace investigator in a favorite **whodunit** book. Now you're curious, how do the investigators solve crimes?

The answer is *forensic science*. This term means science as it relates to the law. The many areas of forensic science can help link people to crimes, even if there are no eyewitnesses. Forensic scientists look at the evidence left at a crime scene and try to figure out what happened there.

tool marks

DNA sample

chemical residue

Evidence can include fingerprints, shoe prints, and fibers. It can include DNA samples from blood and saliva, tool marks, and chemical residue. Often this evidence can be quite small. In the CSI business, this is known as trace evidence. But even the smallest evidence can place a suspect at a crime scene.

Crime scene investigators **analyze** the evidence. Then they try to answer these questions about a crime.

1. What happened?
2. Where and when did it occur?
3. Who are the suspects, and why did they do it?
4. How was the crime done?

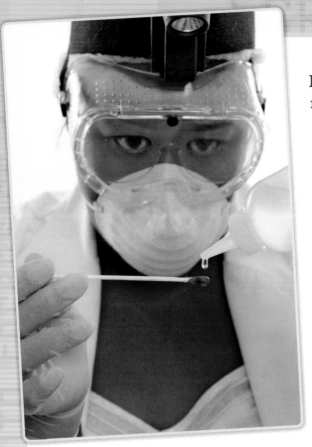

Different kinds of evidence require different kinds of scientists to find the answers to these questions. Forensic scientists specialize in fields such as chemistry, biology, physics, engineering, psychology, and even **entomology** and **botany**.

All these scientists use common sense and old-fashioned observation. They also rely on high-tech equipment and the latest scientific discoveries. Most important, forensic scientists use the scientific method.

Investigators begin by observing the crime scene. They then predict what happened and, if possible, who committed the crime based on the evidence.

Next they test the evidence. Their test results may support their predictions. Or, the results may tell them that their predictions were not correct.

Finally, they draw a conclusion about what happened. They may decide that further testing is required.

In this book series, you'll have a chance to test your own crime-solving talent. You'll do some challenging hands-on forensics activities. Each book in the series covers a specific area of CSI. In addition to this book, *Cool Physical Evidence: What's Left Behind*, be sure to check out:

- *Cool Biological Clues: What Hair, Bones, and Bugs Tell Us*
- *Cool Crime Scene Basics: Securing the Scene*
- *Cool Eyewitness Encounters: How's Your Memory?*
- *Cool Forensic Tools: Technology at Work*
- *Cool Written Records: The Proof Is in the Paper*

Altogether, these books show how crime scene investigators use science to **analyze** evidence and solve crimes.

Whoduzit in Whodunits: Forensic Psychologists

Psychologists study minds and behavior. Forensic psychologists study the minds and behavior of crime suspects. They try to determine motive, or why a person may have committed a crime. They may try to determine whether a person was sane when he or she committed a crime.

F211A

CSI LAB

The Scientific Method

Forensic scientists aren't the only ones who use the scientific method. All scientists do.

The scientific method is a series of steps that scientists follow when trying to answer a question about how the world works. Here are the basic steps of the scientific method.

1. Observe. Pay attention to how something works.

2. Predict. Make a simple statement that explains what you observed.

3. Test. Design an experiment that tests your prediction. You need a good idea of what data to gather during the test. A good test has more than one trial and has controlled variables.

4. Conclude. Compare the data and make a conclusion. This conclusion should relate to your prediction. It will either support the prediction or tell you that your prediction was incorrect.

COOL CSI JOURNAL

Taking notes is important when you collect evidence as a crime scene investigator. Writing down facts helps crime scene investigators remember all the details of a crime scene later, when a crime is tried in court.

At the beginning of each activity in this book, there is a section called "Take Note!" It contains suggestions about what to record in your CSI journal. You

can predict what you think will happen when you test evidence. And you can write down what did happen. Then you can draw a conclusion.

As you do experiments, record things in your journal. You will be working just like a real forensic scientist.

TAKE NOTE!

Get out your CSI journal when you see this box. "Take Note!" may have questions for you to answer about the project. There may be a suggestion about how to look at the project in a different way. There may even be ideas about how to organize the evidence you find. Your CSI journal is the place to keep track of everything!

SAFE SCIENCE

Good scientists practice safe science. Here are some important things to remember.

- **Check with an adult** before you begin any project. Sometimes you'll need an adult to buy materials or help you handle them for a while. For some projects, an adult will need to help you the whole time. The instructions will say when an adult should assist you.

- **Ask for help** if you're unsure about how to do something.

- If something goes wrong, **tell an adult** immediately.

- **Read the list** of things you'll need. Gather everything before you begin working on a project.

- **Don't taste, eat, or drink** any of the materials or the results unless the directions say that you can.

- **Use protective gear.** Scientists wear safety goggles to protect their eyes. They wear gloves to protect their hands from chemicals and possible burns. They wear aprons or lab coats to protect their clothing.

- **Clean up** when you are finished. That includes putting away materials and washing containers, work surfaces, and your hands.

COOL PHYSICAL EVIDENCE: WHAT'S LEFT BEHIND

When you think of crime scene evidence, chances are you mean physical evidence. Physical evidence is any inorganic clue found at a scene. The term *inorganic* means that the evidence isn't from living things, as blood and hair are. Tire prints, fibers, and chemicals are some kinds of physical evidence.

Investigators look for fingerprints at most crime scenes. They know that each person has a **unique** print. Even identical twins

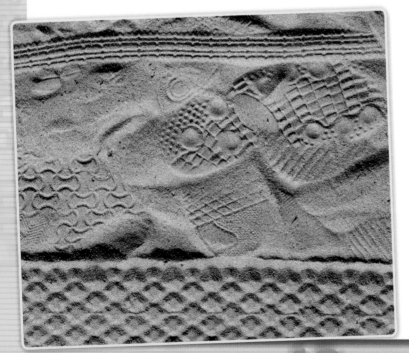

have different prints! So fingerprints help identify suspects. And fingerprint evidence is useful in court because most jury members understand it.

Footprints can help identify people too. Smart criminals know to wear gloves so they won't leave fingerprints behind. But it is trickier to avoid leaving footprints.

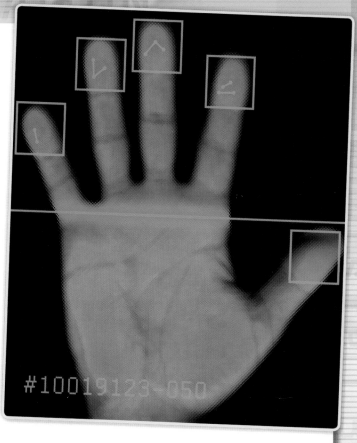

#10019123-050

Crime scene investigators examine footprints for size. They also study the footprints to identify the shoes. Wear marks, such as cracks and worn spots, can connect a print to a suspect's shoe. Compare the bottom of your shoe with the bottom of a friend's shoe. Can you see how each would leave a unique pattern?

Tire prints also contribute important information for crime scene investigators. Was the getaway **vehicle** a small car or a large truck? Which direction did the vehicle come from?

Which way did it go? A good set of tire prints might answer all of these questions. It could also place a suspect's car at the crime scene.

Some types of physical evidence, such as fibers, are even smaller than prints. A fiber is a tiny strand of fabric or carpet. Criminals leave fibers behind at crime scenes. And they pick up fibers there. This transfer is called the Locard Exchange Principle.

Examiners collect fibers from the crime scene. Then they take them to the forensic lab and compare them. They run forensic tests to identify other materials found at crime scenes as well. Sometimes these materials are unknown substances.

Investigators must handle all of this evidence with care! At the crime scene, they collect physical

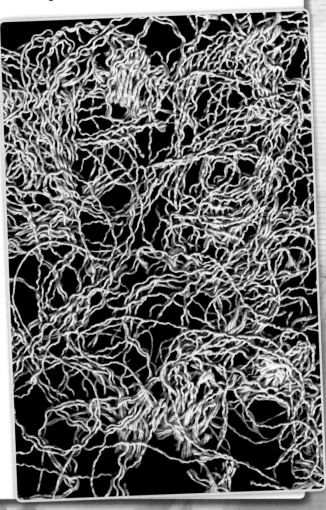

evidence using **forceps**, tape, or vacuums with special filters. Investigators always wear gloves, both for safety and to avoid **contaminating** the evidence. And they take their time when processing the materials. All handlers write careful notes so their work holds up in a court of law.

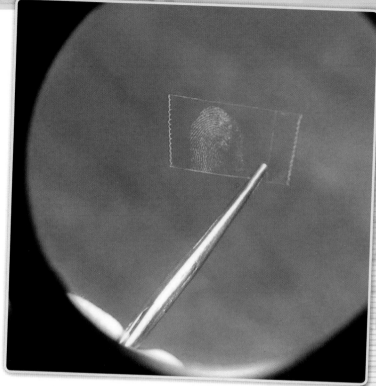

Very small amounts of physical evidence can provide a big break in a **case**. Evidence found in small amounts is called trace evidence. Traces of physical evidence are still very valuable to crime solvers.

The activities in this book will introduce you to the **intriguing** world of forensic science. Have fun trying them, and be sure to keep an open mind. And remember, don't assume that you know more than you do. Let the physical evidence speak for itself. It may tell you all you need to know to solve a crime.

TIRE PRINTS TELL ALL

THE CRIME SCENE: Local garden club members are upset because bike riders zoomed through their flower beds. In other words, the bikers pedaled in their petals! The gardeners expect some help cleaning up the mess. And they know just how to locate the culprits. You could say they plan to track down the bad guys!

In this activity, you'll use miniature tires and ink to study patterns of tire tracks.

MATERIALS

- 20 toy trucks or cars
- inkpad with washable ink
- white paper
- rulers
- friend

TAKE NOTE!

Use your CSI journal to record your tire print keys and your guesses. You can even make your sample tracks there, if you have the space!

1. Divide the toy **vehicles** into two groups. Each person should take a group of 10 vehicles.

2. Make sample tracks from each vehicle in your group. Roll a tire or two from a vehicle across the ink pad. Then "drive" the toy across the paper. Number each sample and keep a key of which vehicle made the prints.

3. Exchange tire print samples and cars with your friend. Try to match each vehicle to its print. Hint: Use your ruler to measure the width of the print. Or look at the **unique** pattern the tire created. Write down your answers.

4. Check each other's work. How did you do?

THINK CSI

Tires can leave three kinds of prints. The prints you created in this exercise are visible prints. In other words, the ink created a track that you can see. **Latent** prints cannot be seen by the naked eye. But investigators use special lights and cameras to see them. Finally, investigators look for **plastic** prints. These 3-D prints form in mud, snow, or sand.

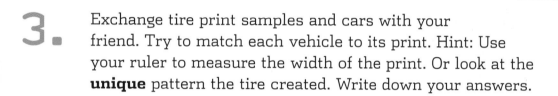

visible

latent

plastic

FOOTPRINT FIGURES

THE CRIME SCENE: This morning someone pulled the fire alarm in your school. It happened before class, when no students were in the building. Your teacher did see a person run past her room. She spied the top of the suspect's head through a window. So, she knows the person is at least five feet (1.5 m) tall.

There are footprints in the mud outside her classroom. Could these belong to the suspect? If so, investigators could match the prints to shoes. The footprints look really small though. Could they belong to someone who's at least five feet (1.5 m) tall?

See how the size of a footprint can predict the height of its maker. All you need is a tape measure, some suspects, and simple mathematics.

MATERIALS

- 6 recruits
- legal-size paper
- pencil
- ruler
- tape measure
- calculator

1. Have your **recruits** remove their shoes.

2. Have each recruit place one foot on a piece of paper.

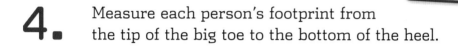

3. Trace around the foot.

4. Measure each person's footprint from the tip of the big toe to the bottom of the heel.

5. Make a table like the one in "Take Note!" Record each person's name and the length of his or her foot.

TAKE NOTE!

Record the measurements from your recruits in a table like this one. Use a calculator to divide each person's foot length by his or her height. Multiply your answers by 100. Be sure to use the same unit of measure for all your measurements.

	Name	Foot length	Height	Foot length ÷ Height	× 100 (results)
1.					
2.					
3.					
4.					
5.					
6.					

Footprint Figures

6. Have each **recruit** stand up straight against a wall. Use the tape measure to measure each person's height. Be sure to use the same unit of measure you used to measure the footprints.

7. Record each person's height in the table.

8. Divide the length of each person's foot by his or her height. Multiply this number by 100. Place the answer in the results column.

9. Review the results in the table. What pattern do you notice when you compare each result to the length of that person's foot?

THINK CSI

Investigators can use the length of a footprint to estimate a suspect's height. They know that foot length is about 15 percent of a person's height. But why does anyone care? A height estimate helps narrow the field of suspects. For example, investigators can eliminate people who are clearly too tall or too short.

MYSTERY MATTER

THE CRIME SCENE: Your math class is practicing measuring by making brownies. The only problem is that the ingredients lost their labels in the cupboard. Now you must identify the substances. Is that baking powder or sugar? How would a crime scene investigator solve this kitchen caper?

In this activity, you'll use chemistry to **analyze** substances.

MATERIALS

- paper or plastic cups
- pen or marker
- eyedropper
- baking soda
- baking powder
- sugar
- cornstarch
- white vinegar
- iodine
- friend

TAKE NOTE!

In your CSI journal, draw tables similar to the sample tables shown on page 24. Use them to record your observations.

ANALYZING KNOWN SUBSTANCES

1. Label the four cups that will hold the baking soda, baking powder, sugar, and cornstarch.

2. Place a small amount of each substance in the proper cup.

3. Observe each substance and describe its look, feel, and smell in the known substances table.

4. Working with one substance at a time, add a few drops of water. Describe the results in the known substances table.

5. Label four new cups. Place a small amount of each substance in its own clean cup. Add a few drops of white vinegar. Describe the results in the known substances table.

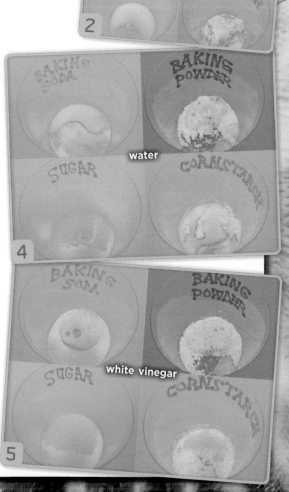

Mystery Matter

6. Label four new cups. Place a small amount of each substance in its own clean cup. Add a few drops of iodine. Describe the results in the known substances table.

7. Your known substances table now contains control data. You can use this data to **analyze** the mystery substances below.

ANALYZING MYSTERY SUBSTANCES

1. Label four cups with the numbers 1, 2, 3, and 4. Have a friend place a small amount of each substance in its own cup. Have the person make a key so you can check your results.

2. Observe each substance and describe its look, feel, and smell in the unknown substances table.

3. Working with one substance at a time, add a few drops of water. Describe the results in the unknown substances table.

CSI TIP

You know that the ingredients you're testing in this activity are safe. After all, they're used to make brownies! So it's okay to touch and smell them. However, in the field, a CSI agent would not do that with unknown substances. And you should never handle in any way a substance you can't identify.

4. Repeat steps 1 and 3 using drops of white vinegar. Your helper should make sure to assign each substance the same number each time. Describe the results in the unknown substances table. Do the same for iodine.

5. Compare the data in your unknown substances and known substances tables. Based on what you know, name the four unknown substances. Check your work against the key. How'd you do?

SAMPLE TABLES

Known Substances

	Observations			Reactions		
Substance	Look	Feel	Smell	Water	Vinegar	Iodine
Baking powder						
Baking soda						
Cornstarch						
Sugar						

Unknown Substances

	Observations			Reactions		
Substance	Look	Feel	Smell	Water	Vinegar	Iodine
Substance 1						
Substance 2						
Substance 3						
Substance 4						

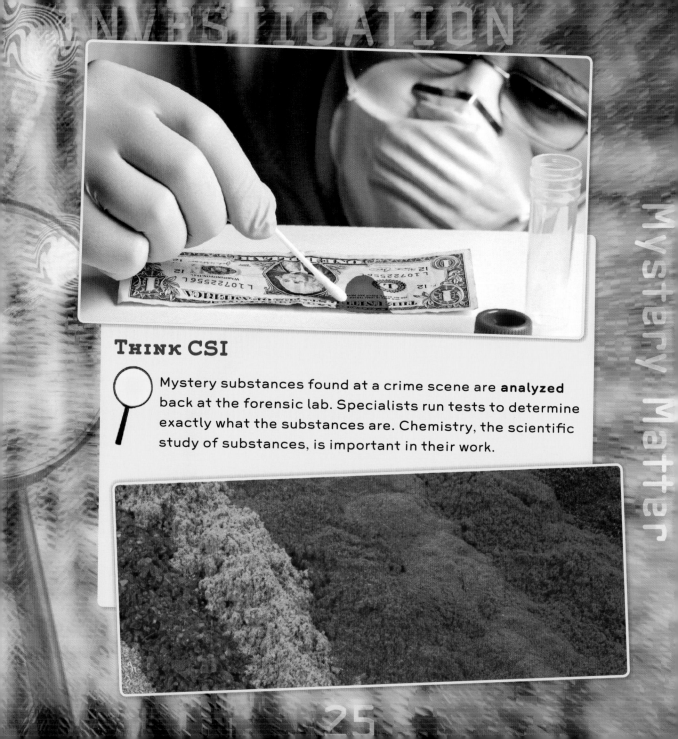

Think CSI

Mystery substances found at a crime scene are **analyzed** back at the forensic lab. Specialists run tests to determine exactly what the substances are. Chemistry, the scientific study of substances, is important in their work.

FINGERPRINT FORENSICS

THE CRIME SCENE: Just last night your dad stocked the cookie jar. Today it's practically empty! He's concerned that his kids aren't eating healthily. So he wants to know who ate the cookies. He knows a handy CSI test to learn who's touched the cookie jar. Will it help answer his question, who stole the cookies from the cookie jar?

In this activity, you'll dust for fingerprints. This process lifts the prints from surfaces so they can be **analyzed.**

MATERIALS

- cocoa
- small paintbrush
- light-colored drinking glass or mug
- transparent tape
- white paper
- pencil
- magnifying glass

TAKE NOTE!

Tape the prints you compare in your CSI journal. Write notes that explain your thinking as you analyze the prints.

DUSTING FOR PRINTS

1. Run your fingers through your hair to gather some natural oils on your fingertips.

2. Press your finger on the glass to create a print.

3. Dip the paintbrush in the cocoa and gently brush it across the print.

4. Place a piece of tape on the fingerprint. Pull up the tape and place it on the paper.

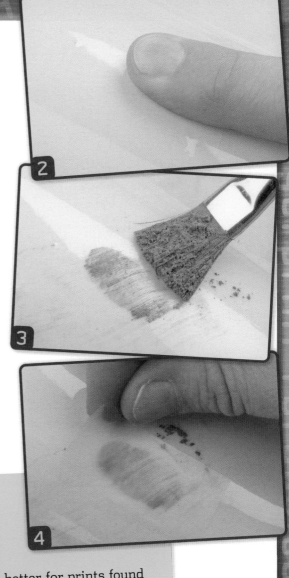

EVEN MORE TO EXPLORE

Cocoa works well when prints are on clear glass or a light-colored surface. But talcum powder works better for prints found on dark-colored surfaces. Repeat the above steps, making a print on a dark surface. Then try white talcum powder as the dusting agent in place of the cocoa. Be sure to place the tape on black paper.

TAKING FINGERPRINT SAMPLES

1. Scribble on a piece of paper with a pencil.

2. Rub your finger in the pencil mark.

3. Put a piece of tape over your finger and press down.

4. Pull the tape off and put it on a piece of paper. You should be able to see the fingerprint.

5. Compare the print with the one you lifted from the glass. Do you see similar patterns?

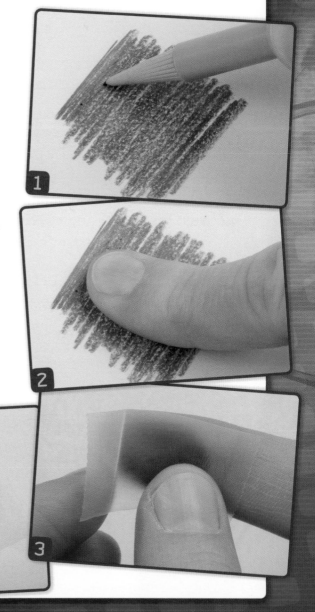

Think CSI

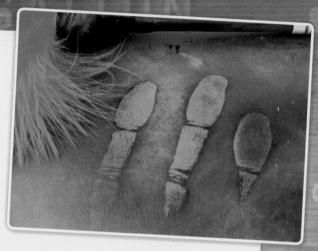

Fingerprints are commonly found at crime scenes. The ridges on everyone's fingers are **unique**. So, investigators can use fingerprints to identify people.

Investigators use the dusting process to locate prints. They then lift the prints and take them to the forensic lab for study. Sometimes they photograph the prints. In the lab, forensic scientists look for patterns, such as loops, arches, and whorls. Today they often use computers to match prints to those taken from suspects.

Whoduzit in Whodunits: Latent Print Examiner

A **latent** print examiner specializes in finding fingerprints that are not visible to the naked eye. This crime lab pro then compares prints from the crime scene with fingerprint exemplars. Exemplars are the samples the investigators hope to match. They might be a prime suspect's prints, for example.

The latent print examiner also enters the prints into the Integrated Automated Fingerprint Identification System. Law enforcement agencies across the country use this fingerprint database. The Federal Bureau of Investigation, or FBI, maintains this important database.

CONCLUSION

The activities featured in this book are the bread and butter of crime scene investigation. You must master these ways of **analyzing** physical evidence to be an ace investigator. But some crime scenes will remain challenging. No two scenes are exactly alike. Evidence can present itself in interesting and unusual ways.

That's when the other books in this series will come in handy. The forensic activities in the Cool CSI series will help you solve even the trickiest crime. And don't forget to use your creativity and your logical mind. As any experienced forensic scientist knows, those are your most valuable tools!

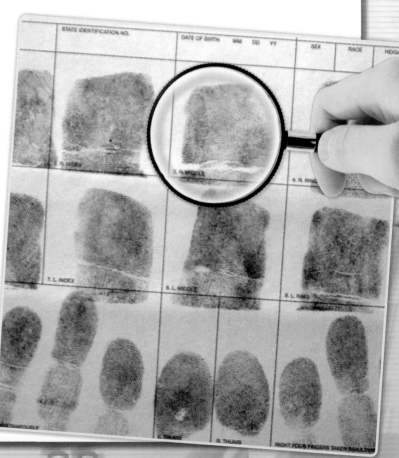

GLOSSARY

analyze – to study the parts of something to discover how it works or what it means.

botany – the study of plants.

case – a situation requiring investigation and consideration by police. Also, the set of arguments made by a lawyer in a court of law.

contaminate – to make something unfit to use by touching it to unwanted elements.

entomology – the study of bugs.

forceps – a tool similar to tweezers used to grasp small or delicate things.

intriguing – fascinating.

latent – not now visible or active, but may become visible or active.

plastic – being a material that is soft enough to mold, but will harden after being molded.

recruit – someone who has been persuaded to join a group.

unique – being the only one of its kind.

vehicle – something used to carry persons or large objects. Examples include cars, trucks, boats, and bicycles.

whodunit – a slang word meaning detective story or mystery story.

WEB SITES

To learn more about the science of forensics, visit ABDO Publishing Company on the World Wide Web at www.abdopublishing.com. Web sites about CSI and forensics are featured on our Book Links page. These links are routinely monitored and updated to provide the most current information available.

INDEX